Pickleball

Less Is More

PICKLEBALL

Less Is More

PAT CARROLL

Vista, CA

Printed in the United States of America

First Printing: January 2018

DEDICATION

I must first thank Martha Bryson, a student who encouraged me several years ago to write a book about Pickleball; and Pat Rider, who encouraged me to establish my business, "Pat's Picklosophy."

Next to thank is Coach Alan Christensen, who taught me how to overcome my tennis techniques and learn how to efficiently accomplish the art of pickleball. The patience and discipline I learned from Alan have influenced every part of my life, and have made me a happier person and a National Champion in singles and doubles competition.

Much thanks goes to the many doubles partners I have played tournaments with throughout the years. You have taught me how to enjoy the game regardless of whether we won or lost. At the top of that list is Phil Dunmeyer, a great partner and the finest gentleman I have ever known – on or off the court.

Perhaps the best student I have taught is Jane Porphir, who stood on the podium at national tournaments many times and frequently fought through challenging draws. Jane's persistence and dedication have been great examples of how to be a true champion, in life and in pickleball. Her assistance in my clinics has been invaluable!

Thank you, Cathy and Steve Brendel, for your help in completing this book, but mostly for your friendship and constant support of my "Picklosophy."

Many thanks to Harry Carpenter for his guidance and encouragement during my writing process.

A special thank you to Bill Dunmeyer for his generous and skilled efforts to reproduce the illustrations in this book to a quality beyond my expectations.

USAPA (USA PICKLEBALL ASSOCIATION) gave me guidance and provided resources for my own personal growth as well as for the growth of pickleball.

And finally and most importantly, my dear Sheila, thank you for the countless hours you have given supporting me at tournaments, working with me in clinics, and sharing 24 years, so far, of life's journey. You are my greatest teacher!

INTRODUCTION

If I had focused on the destination, I'd never have enjoyed the journey. And what a wonderful journey it has been! Since a very young age, I have had a passion for sports, beginning with my 8th grade softball team. I was terrible, but good enough to play right field and hit an occasional single. I also wanted to compete in figure skating, but a teaching pro told my parents, "Don't waste your money; she's too clumsy to be a competitive skater." This broke my heart, but instead of giving up I became determined to prove him wrong. Three years later with the help of another coach, I won both figure and freestyle titles in my region, and finished 6th in the Nationals.

In my senior year of high school, I learned tennis by hitting against the gym wall, and made the team. When I was 20 I discovered bowling and became a professional bowler after two years of coaching. I enjoyed coaching junior bowlers and also won a few tournaments. Later, my passion for tennis returned, and by age 35 I was a top competitor in the midwestern states. By age 40, I was recruited from Iowa to California to teach tennis full time. I was trained and certified and found that teaching the sport I loved to others was actually more fulfilling than my passion for competing. After a few years teaching tennis, I changed to a marketing career which took me away from tennis and competition, but involved a lot of the teaching skills I had developed through the years. After an early retirement, my passion returned and I began competing in the National Senior Tennis Circuit, where I gained a national ranking of "25."

These experiences gave me a deep understanding of how important it is to believe in myself regardless of what others might tell me; but more importantly, it gave me true compassion for the player who appears clumsy, or doesn't achieve goals as quickly as most of their peers. This was my story. The key for me was finding a coach who recognized my passion and believed in me. At some level I knew that everything I had experienced in my life up to now was getting me ready for my greatest passion of all, pickleball! I discovered this great game in 2002 and walked away from tennis in 2003 to devote all my time and energy to learning, competing, and teaching. I served for one year as Marketing Director of the USA Pickleball Association and have promoted pickleball as a USAPA Ambassador since 2005.

After two years of training from the best player/coach in the US, Alan Christensen, I began teaching classes and private lessons, and in 2010 I started my business "Pat's Picklosophy," teaching and traveling throughout the United States with my home base in San Diego County. Alan taught me to keep my technique and strategies simple and it worked. I won eight National titles in Singles, Doubles, and Mixed Doubles, and many of my students have also stood on the podium at the Nationals.

The contents of this book include everything I have learned in my 15 years playing Pickleball. All it takes to succeed is a lot of patience, discipline, and commitment. Forget about a destination; there will always be more to achieve.

Enjoy your journey!

Pat Carroll
December 2017

Contents

PART THREE *"The Journey to the Top of the Podium"*......59

PART ONE
Laying a Solid Foundation

It is essential that you learn and use efficient technique on all shots. This is the focus of part one, and will help you discover ways you might be complicating your techniques, and sabotaging your success.

There is no shortcut to playing winning pickleball. Just as a house without a solid foundation will eventually crumble, a player without good basics will, at some point, become stuck. It's an easy "trap" to get caught in. Hitting the ball over the net and into the court comes quickly and easily for most, giving them the illusion that they can play the game without much attention to technique, strategy, or movement.

As you begin to play against higher skilled opponents, points will frequently include twenty or more shots. Also, those low hard shots no longer work, and often end up in the loss of the point. This is where players hit a wall if they don't have good fundamentals and strategies. When this occurs, it is time to get back to basics. In some cases, a complete reconstruction will be necessary. It is much easier to take the time in the beginning to develop efficient techniques and movement.

Whether you are a new player, or one of the many players who have become "stuck," the following pages will simplify your shots, improve your footwork, and add consistency and control to your game. Most importantly, these techniques will promote better balance and reduce risk of injury dramatically.

1 EQUIPMENT

Shoes: Wearing the proper shoes is essential, and tennis shoes are the proper choice. They afford the most lateral protection from twisting an ankle; optimum cushioning of the sole; proper ability to slide and pivot; and wear well.

Running shoes do not provide adequate side support and the soles grip too much, which can result in falling or turning an ankle.

Cross training shoes offer something for every sport, but they are not optimum for any sport.

Even though the bottoms of your old tennis shoes are not worn through, the shoe has a finite life. After the shoes have been flexed over and over the tops lose their ability to support your feet and ankles properly. Some experts claim that you should not keep them for more than six months even if they look like they are in good condition.

Paddles: I recommend a minimum weight of 9 oz. This assures that the paddle head is heavier than the handle. A heavier head promotes the quickest transfer of weight through the hit, and results in more control with less effort. Some believe that a light paddle is best. A lighter paddle enables a quicker wrist motion, mobility, and paddle speed; however, I believe that: a) if you are in position, you don't need to move the paddle far, b) wrist motion adds another degree of difficulty, and c) the hitting motion is only a short punch/push, which favors a heavier paddle. "Smart" pickleball is less smacking and more control.

Note: I have developed a paddle which has optimum balance and weight for maximum performance. It is manufactured by ZZT Sports to my specifications, and is available only through Pat's Picklosophy (*pickleballpat@yahoo.com*). It's called the "Less Effort" paddle.

2 GRIPS AND READY POSITION

Recommended GRIP for all shots: shake hands with your paddle, making sure that your thumb and index finger are touching.

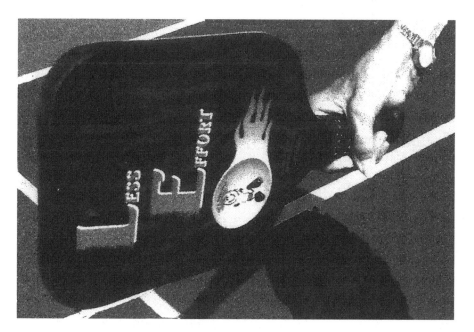

Body position/stance recommended to prepare for all shots: knees bent, shoulders over toes, and feet slightly wider than the shoulders, with paddle backhand-ready.

The "COMFORT ZONE" (hitting zone) for contacting the ball is ideally one foot in front of the body, and no more than one foot to either side of the body.

Drill: without a paddle, catch balls off the bounce with both hands. Be aware of your body position at the catch, your balance, and that you are SQUARE to the ball (turning the body or a long step creates difficulty in recovering for the next shot; moreover, it can result in injuries).

3 FOOTWORK
"DA AGONY OF DA FEET!"

Perhaps the MOST NEGLECTED part of learning this game is the most important part—FOOTWORK! No matter how great your dinks, volleys, and ground strokes, lazy/sluggish/slow/ sloppy footwork will frequently result in loss of the point, and ultimately keep you "stuck" at your current skill level.

Making less errors and hitting with power are predicated on your body being in a balanced stance and positioned to hit the ball in your power/ comfort zone, which is one foot in front and no farther than one foot to either side.

Use the following for getting your feet moving efficiently.

- KEEP THE FEET ACTIVE! (3 steps per second during a point.) Planting the feet is a common error, especially while at the 7 ft. line. Dance!

- PRACTICE AND "MASTER" LATERAL MOVEMENT. "Be "square," and be "a winner." This is not a difficult adjustment and can be practiced at home. Keeping the feet square to the shot at contact improves consistency, and eliminates potential foot-faults at the 7 ft. line.

> *TIP: Taking a step "while" hitting a shot or "stepping across your body" to play a ball complicates the shot by adding unnecessary motion (of the feet and shoulders). This extra motion requires recovery time and takes you out of position for the next shot.*

- POSITION YOUR FEET to contact the ball in front of your body within your comfort zone for every shot. Lazy feet cause "reaching" for balls, which results in loss of control and injuries.
- MOVE WITH THE BALL! Stay even with the ball when it is on the opponent's side of the court, or within the shaded area from the ball to the corners of your side of the court (see Part Three—Shading, pp70-73).
- **Several small steps are more efficient for getting your body to the proper position than two or three long steps**. Small steps allow for fine-tuning your feet to your comfort zone, and reduces chances of injury.

*Crossing over
complicates the shot*   *Staying square
makes recovery easy*

FOREHAND:

BACKHAND:

DRILL: To train your feet for smaller steps; with knees bent, do 30 steps in place in 10 seconds. Then try the same drill with lateral steps, back and forth at the 7 ft. line on the court (this can also be practiced at home).

TIP: Next time you are on the court, listen to your feet; make sure they are moving at the rate of 3 steps per second during a point. You'll be amazed at how much quicker you are moving and how much easier each shot becomes.

THE BEST NEWS OF ALL: active footwork improves physical conditioning and weight loss—you'll get to shop for a smaller wardrobe!

THE MOST IMPORTANT FOOTWORK RULE TO REMEMBER:

"DON'T GIVE UP TOO SOON!"

MAKE A COMMITMENT TO CONTINUE MOVING FOR THE BALL UNTIL IT HAS BOUNCED TWICE

You have much more time than you think to get to that shot. Moving your feet and refusing to give up on the shot until the ball has bounced a second time will reveal to you that you can get to far more shots than you thought.

4 MORE ABOUT FOOTWORK

HOW IMPORTANT IS IT REALLY?

Efficient footwork is as important to pickleball as the foundation is to building a house; without it, damage and deterioration will occur prematurely. The following are the most common errors and consequences of poor footwork:

- Feet become planted in one place, resulting in slow movement to shots when needed. Example: While approaching an intersection at 5 MPH when the light turns green, acceleration from the same spot is several times faster than for a stopped car. The same is true in pickleball; if your feet remain active at the moment the opponent hits a shot, you will be amazed at how many more shots you can get to with less effort.

- Paddle moves first toward shot, causing reaching outside the comfort zone, and lack of control. Moving your feet first to the shot makes it possible to hit within your comfort zone on most shots. Not only will this result in more control, you will make shots with good balance. Those who reach rather than move their feet need to master 20 or 30 different shots, instead of 6 or 7.

- After continuous planting and reaching, the body begins to break down. Leaning forward to reach shots stresses the back. Leaning to the right or left stresses the upper leg muscles, hips, and knees. Planting the heels during points stresses the tendons in the feet and ankles.

Unfortunately, no matter what age or skill level you are, footwork is not a priority to most players. After all, it's a small court which appears to be very easy to cover, especially when playing doubles. The younger players with less miles on their bodies can survive longer before injuries begin to occur; but those injuries will eventually happen for all who fail to develop efficient footwork.

5 BASIC SHOTS FROM THE 7-FOOT LINE

Two Types of Shots

SWINGS:

- Mainly used for return of serve & overhead

- Circular motion demands perfect timing

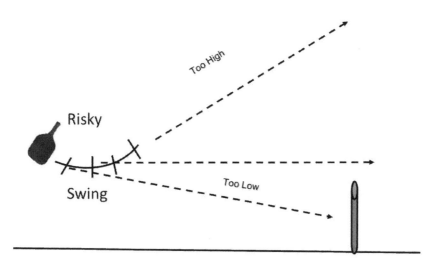

PUSHES:

- Used for dinks, volleys, & drop shots

- More accurate—pushed straight to target

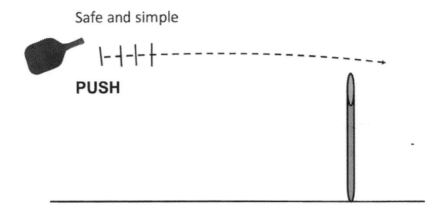

Safe and simple

PUSH

Dinks

Power shots when the opponents are at the 7 ft. line continue upward beyond the net, making volleys easy. Soft shots (dinks and drop shots) will drop below the net, bouncing even with the opponent's feet, creating a much more difficult shot.

A dink is a PUSH (keep paddle in front, with NO BACKSWING)!

Finish with tip of paddle still pointing below horizontal— USE A "REVERSE HINGE" at wrist!

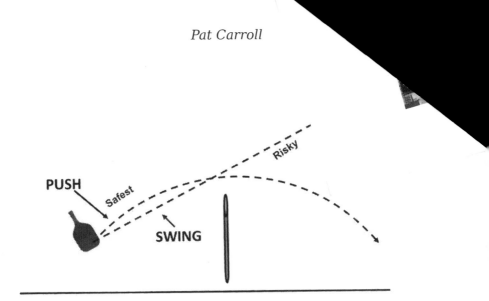

"HINGING" is bending wrist toward the shot, and causes you to pop the ball upward.

AVOID SPIN! It adds considerable difficulty to your shot and is usually ineffective against better players.

Dinking Do's and Don'ts

- Keep paddle tip lower and ahead of handle at contact.
- PUSH and then STOP the paddle after hit. Keep the paddle facing the direction you want the ball to go.
- Avoid "hinging" (breaking the wrist after the hit).
- Avoid a follow-through motion.
- Keep your eyes on the ball throughout contact.

The Dink is a key shot when all 4 players are at the 7-foot line. If placed within the non-volley zone, the opponents have few choices other than to respond with a dink. In high skill level games, points frequently consist of 20 or more dinks, until someone either hits into the net or too high. Patience is required to hit "one more dink" until the opportunity comes to end the point.

Practice dinking drills until you can hit 30 in a row into the non-volley zone, forehand and backhand.

Volleys—The "easiest" shot in pickleball!

Generally a PUSH, except on balls "above" your shoulders.
Begin with paddle in the backhand ready position (70% of volleys and dinks will be backhands).

Position paddle 6"- 12" in front of your body, NO BACKSWING!

Keep paddle handle pointing toward your hip (to avoid "inside-out" shots);

A common error on the backhand volley is to lift the elbow and hit too far in front; keep elbow close to the body for better control and power.

Push in direction you want the ball to go.

Maintain a square paddle; finish with paddle still within your target line as moving paddle downward risks hitting into the net.

Drill: At 7-foot line, hit controlled volleys to shoulder height of drilling partner(s). Goal is 20 in a row, straight, and from both sides cross-court.

Drill: Hit volleys to deep person's feet (to keep opponents back).

TIP: Avoid hitting "to" your opponents; make them reach!

6 THE SERVE

The purpose is 'to get the ball in play,' not to ACE your opponent.

- Start close to the center line, with body sideways to net. Stationary feet will prevent unwanted variation in serve; a shift of weight from back to front provides plenty of power.
- Hold and release ball IN FRONT OF FORWARD FOOT (a slight lift of the ball rather than a drop gives more time to bring your paddle to the ball).
- Keep eyes on ball, keeping head down until after striking the ball (don't look up until your serving arm has touched your chin).
- Contact the ball below your waist.

- The head of your paddle must be below your wrist at impact.

- Follow through, extending arm toward the target.

The most important strategy is to serve DEEP into the service court.

> *TIP: A higher serve at least 4-6 feet over the net is most effective, since it requires the receiver to supply all the power on the return. Serving hard allows the receiver to "feed" on your power, giving them an easier and deeper return.*

Drill: serve 10 balls to a spot on the court (keep track of percentages); repeat several times. The goal is to serve 100% in the court, and at least 70% DEEP in the court.

7 RETURN OF SERVE

THE MOST IMPORTANT SHOT IN THE GAME!

- Stand at baseline or behind, not inside (unless you know server is weak).

- A good service return requires a backswing and follow-through from a sideways position.

- Move your feet to contact the ball in front of the forward foot and lean into the shot at contact. Leaning into your shot promotes forward movement to the line.

- The recommended return of serve is the FOREHAND. This is because the natural rotation of the body during the follow-through promotes quicker movement to the line. Returning with the backhand requires a sideways position throughout the shot, resulting in loss of nearly a second in approaching the 7-foot line.

- Come rapidly forward immediately after hitting the ball. The goal is to get to the line before the 3rd shot is hit.

- Returning DEEP is the most important aspect of the serve return. Higher returns (at least 4-5 feet above the net) landing deep in the court provide more time for you to come forward, keeping the serving team back. Also, the ball bounces higher, forcing the serving team farther back, making a more difficult third shot.

The service return places the receiving team (or individual, if a singles game) in position to prevent the serving team (or individual) from scoring. Why is it so important? If not executed well it puts the serving team in position to win the point easily. A consistently deep return is of utmost importance.

Drill: return the serve down the middle to within 4 feet of the baseline, rushing to the line before the serving team has struck the 3rd shot. Keep score, giving yourself a point if both depth and speed to the line are successful, or give the server a point if not. Practice at least half-an-hour per week exclusively on return of serve drills—it'll improve your game dramatically!

8   DROP SHOTS

The drop shot is a soft shot, made from any place behind the 7-foot line, low over the net and into the opponent's 7-foot zone. When standing at the 7-foot line, it's called a "dink" (see pages 16-18).

The drop shot is the serving team's best third-shot selection for safely advancing into scoring position at the 7-foot line. A successful drop shot will bounce low at the opponent's feet, making it difficult for them to respond with a forcing shot.

TECHNIQUE OF THE DROP SHOT IS SIMPLE

- Using the same technique as the dink, keep the paddle in front with the tip down.
- The difference is in the footwork. Since the ball is usually traveling faster, position yourself farther behind the bounce. This assures contact in front of the body and results in more control.
- It is important to contact the drop shot within your "comfort zone," just like the dink.

- Contact should be made well behind the bounce, while the ball is descending rather than ascending.

THE MOST COMMON ERRORS IN DROP SHOTS ARE:

- Taking a backswing instead of keeping the paddle in front. The backswing will generate power that you don't want for this soft shot.
- Following through upward after contact.
- Lifting the body during the push instead of staying down will increase the degree of difficulty.

> TIP: If you don't follow the drop shot to the 7-ft line, you've wasted a good opportunity to score.

Drill: Make at least 5 drops in a row from mid-court, then from back-court. Then serve, hit a drop shot from the return and follow the ball in to the 7-ft line (repeat several times). It takes many hours to master this shot. Be persistent!

9   THE LOB

A seemingly easy, but very-high-risk shot selection

Lobs from the 7-foot line can be very effective with practice, and much easier to execute than lobs from the back court.

Lobs (at the 7-foot line)

- Prepare to hit ball exactly as you would a dink.
- Use a PUSH motion when you hit the lob, lifting the ball above opponents' reach.
- Deception is part of the success.
- Hitting over opponent's backhand shoulder is ideal.

Lobs from the back court, however, are extremely difficult and very risky.

This lob is usually a defensive shot intended to give the player in the back court time to approach to the 7-foot line. It is a last resort shot, recommended only if you are unable to get into position for a drop shot. If you can't keep that ball in front of you, then take a backswing and LIFT that ball to the sky—then you might want to pray!

Lobs from the back court

* Requires a backswing, with a follow-through toward the sky.
* If hit short, it sets up the opponent for an overhead.

Drill: Practice with a chair set 5 feet in front of opponents' baseline, then bounce the ball on your baseline and hit a lob, lifting the ball high enough to clear the opponents' highest reach, clear the chair, and stay in bounds.

PART TWO
"What Are You Thinking?!"

---

*Ninety percent of your success depends
on your mental game.*

Now that you have a solid foundation of efficient technique on all shots and good, well balanced footwork, you are ready to begin the most challenging part of the game: what shot to choose, and where to hit it?

Part Two introduces more than 50 aspects of the game to know and understand in order to quickly recognize and respond to your opponent's shot, and reply with your smartest shot and target. Every shot from your opponent will demand a split-second decision, and every decision is likely to be a different one. In a point involving 20 or more shots, the best players maintain patience and discipline, and the mental ability to keep the ball in play until either the opponent makes an error, or the opportunity to hit a winning shot occurs. This is a big order, and requires much study and practice.

10   THE MENTAL SIDE OF PLAYING WELL

- Focus (mentally) on THE BALL rather than opponents!

- Forget mistakes—say, "OOPS!" instead of "sorry…."; then, think "NEXT!"

- Negative self-talk wastes energy, and promotes defeat.

- Stay positive with partner.

- HAVE A PLAN! There are three strategies (plans) you MUST KNOW to play successfully:

  ▸ GET TO THE LINE ASAP.

  ▸ KEEP YOUR OPPONENTS AWAY FROM THE LINE AS MUCH AS POSSIBLE.

  ▸ PROTECT YOUR MIDDLE.

MORE ABOUT THE "MENTAL GAME"

The conscious mind is only capable of thinking of one thing at a time. Perhaps the biggest mental mistake players make is trying to remember and apply ALL of the information from this book at once.

The subconscious mind is capable of remembering an infinite amount of information. So, how do we record all of this book's information into the subconscious mind? PRACTICE, of course!

Repetition on the practice court of each drill shown in the shaded areas of this book will eventually move into the subconscious memory, and become a habit during play.

Since you can only focus on one thing consciously, it is best to consciously focus simply on watching the ball. If you find that you are neglecting to use all the strategies and techniques during play, then more practice is needed to record them into your subconscious memory.

GOOD NEWS! You can practice mentally while off the court. Just focus on the skill you want to improve, imagining yourself doing it efficiently and successfully over and over again. You will be amazed at how well this works when practiced regularly. To learn more about this practice technique, I recommend the e-book, "Pickleball, the Mental Side," by Harry Carpenter (available at Amazon Books). This book raised my level of play dramatically. He also has published a CD, which is a great aid for playing in the zone.

TIP: Wherever you are on the court; and whatever shot you choose, "FOCUS ON THE BALL" (try seeing the holes in the ball; and don't look up until you've seen the ball connect with your paddle. This requires discipline; but is absolutely necessary to become a more accomplished player)!

11 UNDERSTANDING YOUR OPTIONS

Before you choose a shot, you need to understand the levels of risk and difficulty. Shots are listed in the order of their importance. Highest difficulty or risk is a 10.

SHOT SELECTION	DIFFICULTY	RISK
Return of Serve	2	2
Dink	2	2
Drop Shot		
From mid-court	5	4
From back-court	8	6
Volley	2	2
Serve	4	2
Lob		
From 7-foot line	5	6
From back-court	9	9
Overhead	7	7

12 CHOOSING YOUR TARGET

Choosing the middle (between opponents) lowers risk, creates confusion, and simplifies angles for your next shot. Placing your shot even with the feet of one or both opponents makes it even more difficult to return.

TARGET	DIFFICULTY	RISK
Middle	2	2
Sidelines	7	7
Even with opponent's feet	7	4
HEIGHT OVER NET		
12 inches or less	6	5
1 foot to 3 feet		
If opponents are back	3	5
If opponents are at the 7-foot line	3	8
10 feet or higher	6	9

The Middle: The Best Target 90% of the Time

Pat's Picklosophy's word for the middle is "Mildred." She is your third teammate, and is always standing between your two opponents. Hitting most shots to "Mildred" simplifies your playing plan and will result in far less errors and more points won.

There are three good reasons to choose the middle:

- No risk of hitting the shot wide.
- Your opponents need to decide who will take the shot.
- Shots hit by opponents from the middle have less angle, and are easier to reach.

Although a shot hit to the middle of the opponents' court might not be a winner, it frequently is a setup toward making your next shot a winner. Opponents usually end up reaching for the middle shot, which causes less control and over hitting.

This doesn't mean you should never hit shots to the sidelines of the court. Wait for the opening on the sideline to hit to and hit to the middle until that opening occurs. If your opponents realize you are hitting most shots to "Mildred," they will be more protective of the middle, and leave more openings on the sidelines for winners.

Make "Mildred" your best friend and enjoy your winning results!

13 FIVE-POINT CHECKUP FOR EVERY SHOT

All five points are critical to a successful shot, and are completed within 1 or 2 seconds. If a shot results in an error, or the opponent hits a winner on the next shot, at least one of the points has not been successful.

1. **RECOGNITION** This is the ability to identify the direction, pace, spin, and height of the coming shot, as well as what shot to choose (forehand, backhand, dink, volley, drop, overhead, etc.), and my best location on the court for my chosen shot.

2. **PREPARATION** and

3. **MOVEMENT** Once recognition is processed, the paddle begins preparing for the chosen shot, and feet begin moving toward the chosen location for the shot.

4. **EXECUTION** After recognition has been instant and accurate, and preparation and movement have been as fast as possible, executing the chosen shot requires a

thorough understanding of best targets and most efficient technique of the shot.

5. **RECOVERY** Returning to the "ready position" with the paddle asap while moving to the best position on the court for the opponent's next shot with a thorough understanding of "shading" and who is responsible for the middle of your court (see Part Three—Shading, pp70-73).

Once the weak points are identified, focused practice is required to move more smoothly through the point.

Some common weaknesses are:

- Not enough focus on the dynamics in point #1, which will slow the remaining 4 points.
- Poor footwork: planting the feet at the 7-foot line, failure to set up before the shot, continuing to move the feet during the shot.
- Lack of awareness of the ready position of the paddle between points.
- Poor execution of shots due to not enough practice. Individual shot improvement seldom occurs from

playing games. Specific shots will improve with commitment to drilling regularly.

- Admiring shots before totally recovering. Recovery nearly always requires quick movement.

When you are failing to play at your highest ability, review the 5 points asking yourself if you're slow or sloppy throughout the process. Remember the initials, R.P.M.E.R. Using this exercise can be the difference between having a good day on the court and having a GREAT day on the court.

14 BACKHANDS VS FOREHANDS

There is, in my opinion, a huge fallacy regarding the subject of forehands. I mean that some players think a shot in question should always be taken by the partner in position to hit a forehand. Yielding to the forehand on shots just because it's a forehand frequently creates poor court coverage and results in lost points. Also, MOST errors are made with forehands rather than backhands.

Return Of Serve

The forehand is the preferred shot for returning serves because most players have more power and are more comfortable on the forehand side. Also, the backswing is longer (it's struck by the back arm if the returner is standing sideways), and the player is hitting from the 'paddle' side of their body. Also, the body can move forward more quickly and naturally from the forehand follow-through position. A common error in the forehand return is to strike the ball too close to the body. Contacting the ball ahead of the front foot creates a forward balance, and results in both power and control.

IMPORTANT: Since the main goal in return of serve is to return DEEP, power is not as important as control. In fact, a higher, softer forehand returned DEEP gives the returner more time to approach; and the server has not only been forced farther behind the court, but also has a much more difficult shot and a longer distance to the 7-foot line.

Shots Other Than Return of Serve

Players who have spent time practicing the backhand can make very consistent, well-controlled shots. Since the backhand is the best choice for all shots from the 'paddle hip' to the opposite side of the body, this leaves only 30% of the remaining shots for the forehand side. The main reason for added control on the backhand is because the body won't allow a backswing, since the body should remain square to all shots after the return of serve. The forehand is more complicated due to the ability to take a backswing and frequently hit with too much power.

> TIP: Backhands in pickleball are much easier to control and less complicated than forehands. Players who choose backhands whenever possible will be less tempted to over-hit, will play better, and win more!

15 "BETWEEN THE POINTS" MATTERS

Time between points is usually between 10 and 20 seconds. In doubles play*, what do you do with that time?

What NOT to do (the Problem)

If you've won the previous point and/or are ahead in score, you might praise each other, and feel increased confidence, with no discussion on what your plan might be for the next point. This can be very risky, especially if the opponents are using their "between the points" time wisely.

If you've lost the point, disappointment sets in, and there usually is little or no communication. This is the worst use of time that could have been used to make adjustments and improve play for the remainder of the game.

What TO DO (the Solution)

If you are guilty of either of the above, the solution seems simple: just use the time to discuss the NEXT point. The question is, "How do we determine what needs to be discussed?"

First, you need to **immediately recognize what's working or not working**. If it's working, reinforce your plan through repetition ("Nice deep serve, let's keep up our soft shots, and continue to keep them back." Or, "Nice try; let's keep on playing the middle."). If it's not working, is it due to your poor shots or flawed strategy? Perhaps you are giving the opponents easy to play shots and need to determine weak areas to challenge them more ("We're giving the strongest player too many shots; let's hit more shots to the weaker player." Or, "They like hard shots; let's make sure to play mostly soft shots."). A good plan can work for a few points, then become less effective and need some more adjusting. This is why it is important to communicate after every point.

Second, if the opponents are hitting frequent winners, ask yourselves what YOU are doing that is making their winners possible, and agree together on the solution ("I'm hitting my shots too high; I have to aim lower." Or, "We have to choose a drop shot on the 3rd shot instead of a lob or hard drive." Or, "Every time we hit a short return, they hit a winner.").

In Conclusion

Acquiring the DISCIPLINE to apply these solutions to the short time between points is difficult, and **needs to be practiced as much as every other aspect of the game**. Knowing what to discuss is the difference between winning and losing. There is NO TIME for emotions or regrets between points. Stay positive in your discussions, and replace the word "sorry" with a quick "oops." The best word and focus between points to remember is "NEXT."

> *In singles play, the conversation must be with yourself, avoiding looking back and always renewing your plan.*

16 UNDERSTANDING THE ZONES FOR CREATING WINNERS

THE IDEAL STRATEGY IS TO PUSH YOUR OPPONENTS BACK TO ZONE 4 OR 5, AND GET YOURSELF AND YOUR PARTNER TO ZONE 1 ASAP

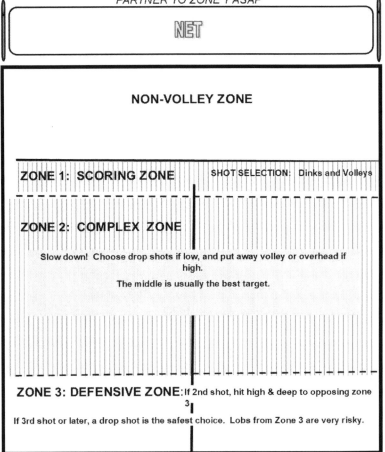

NET

NON-VOLLEY ZONE

ZONE 1: SCORING ZONE   SHOT SELECTION: Dinks and Volleys

ZONE 2: COMPLEX ZONE

Slow down! Choose drop shots if low, and put away volley or overhead if high.

The middle is usually the best target.

ZONE 3: DEFENSIVE ZONE: If 2nd shot, hit high & deep to opposing zone 3.

If 3rd shot or later, a drop shot is the safest choice. Lobs from Zone 3 are very risky.

ZONE 4: "TROUBLE" ZONE: Same plan as Zone 3, only much more difficult.

ZONE 5: "DOUBLE-TROUBLE" ZONE:

Non-Volley Zone

Footwork is the most important element of making shots within the Non-Volley Zone. Step into this zone quickly, with both feet if possible to provide optimum stability and control; followed by a quick retreat to the Scoring Zone.

Zone 1: Scoring Zone

Shot selection: dinks and volleys. Frequently, choosing a set-up dink to force your opponent to reach will result in an opportunity to follow their return shot with an easy winner.

Zone 2: Complex Zone

Slow down (avoid rushing and over hitting). Going for winners from this zone is very risky. Most shots from the Complex Zone are approach shots. Choose a volley or overhead if high. If your partner is at the Scoring Zone, choose diagonal shots rather than straight shots to prevent the opponents' hitting behind your partner and away from you. Otherwise, the middle is usually the best target.

Zone 3: Defensive Zone

If return of serve (2nd shot), hit high and deep to zone 3 of opponents' court. If 3rd shot or later, a drop shot is the safest choice. Lobs from Zone 3 are very risky.

Zone 4: "Trouble Zone"

Same plan as zone 3, only much more difficult.

Zone 5: "Double-Trouble Zone"

When caught in zone 5 it is difficult to keep the ball in front for a drop shot; so try a high lob to the middle, get into at least zone 2 if the lob is a safe one, and work your way to zone 1.

17 CONTROVERSIAL STRATEGIES

Simple & Efficient vs. Risky & Complicated

FOOTWORK

SIMPLE & EFFICIENT—Active feet moving with small steps toward the ball results in good balance and a quick recovery.

RISKY & COMPLICATED—Planting the feet and reaching with the paddle results in less control and excessive stress on the body which leads to injuries.

FOREHANDS vs. BACKHANDS

Although the forehand is the best choice for returning the serve, errors at the 7-foot line are 85% on the forehand. Backhands are more controlled, with less power, which works best at the line. Forehands are more complicated due to the temptation to over hit.

Positioning the paddle in the middle of the body pointed toward the net is actually being "ready for NOTHING." Since the backhand is the best choice for shots made from even with the paddle hip over, a "backhand ready" position is the most efficient position at the line.

When the ball comes high, the forehand can be struck for more power; but the risk is in over-hitting. A well-placed shot is the most frequent winner vs. extreme power.

STAYING BACK ON THE THIRD SHOT

One player at the line is better than NONE at the line. If your partner consistently chooses a drop shot, you are safe to go to the line ahead of him/her. To avoid risk, the drop shot should be placed diagonally, to the opponent who has no "hole" to hit through. If it is placed to the same side as the hitter, the opponent sees the "hole", and can hit the shot through the middle behind the in partner, and away from the dropper.

If your partner prefers to "pound" the third shot, it is too risky to approach the line. This reduces the opportunities to make winning shots dramatically.

DINKS AND VOLLEYS SHOULD BE "PUSHES" vs. "SWINGS"

Shots with no backswing or follow-through are most efficient and result in far more accuracy. Taking a step while hitting a dink or volley complicates the shot, and frequently adds unwanted pace to the shot. Move to the shot and set the feet, using only the paddle to make the shot.

SPIN: TOPSPIN AND SLICE CAN BE VERY RISKY AND COMPLICATED

Since the USAPA rules forbid altering the slick surface of the paddle to generate spin, attempting spin with a regulation paddle requires exaggerating the backswing and follow-through. This results in less control and more errors.

PLACING YOUR SHOT WITH A MINIMUM OF PADDLE MOTION IS MORE EFFICIENT, EVEN WHEN HITTING HIGH SHOTS FOR WINNERS.

> To summarize, many players use "selective memory" to justify using the complicated and risky strategies listed above. It is a human tendency to remember the two times their

high risk shots were winners, and forget the dozen times they resulted in errors. Highly skilled players lose many points and games due to lack of the patience and discipline to select efficient shots instead of the popular flashy shots.

RATE YOUR SKILLS

The following three inventories will help you identify your weaknesses and strengths. Follow directions at the end to determine your skill level.

18 DECISION-MAKING INVENTORY

How well you make decisions when playing is one of the most important aspects of playing good pickleball; but it is also one of the most difficult areas to self-assess. The following questions will help with your decision-making inventory. Score yourself as follows:

Always-5, Usually-4, Sometimes-3, Seldom-2, Never-1.

Add your scores together; your skill level in this category is: 14-3.0, 18-3.5, 23-4.0, 28-4.5, 35- 5.0

	My targets are well inside the court; mostly to the middle of the court so that I keep a high percentage of balls in.
	I usually choose well-placed shots vs. overpowering shots.
	I choose a drop shot to approach the 7ft. line (if opponents are in).

	I am aware that a backhand vs. forehand is usually a more controlled shot.
	I intend to protect or set up my partner with every shot.
	I usually bounce a low ball, and return it with a dink.
	I hit forcing shots (taking my opponent off balance) when the ball comes high to me.
	I choose the shot that is easy to execute rather than the difficult one (willing to wait for an easier shot before trying for a winner).
	I am patient and disciplined, willing to hit 30+ dinks every point.
	TOTAL

19 SHOT-MAKING INVENTORY

SHOTS ARE LISTED IN ORDER OF THEIR IMPORTANCE.
Score 1(very poor) through 5(very accurate and consistent)
Note: less baseline lobs scores higher.

Add scores together; your shot-making skill level is: 24-3.0,
28-3.5, 32-4.0, 35-4.5, 38-5.0

	Return of Serve (high over the net and deep to center). A forehand return instead of backhand can get me to the line sooner.
	Dink (1 ft. above the net, pushed softly into the NV zone).
	Drop Shot (a long dink, allowing more space before hit, and a longer push to 1 ft. above the net) Not a swing!
	Volley (push outward, not down; using control vs. power).
	Serve (high & deep is more effective than low & hard).
	Lob from 7-ft line (best over opponent's backhand shoulder).
	Lob from baseline: never scores-5, seldom-4, sometimes-3, usually-2, always-1
	Lobs from the baseline are highly risky, and should be used only as a last resort.
	Overhead (usually, stay square & hit a high volley instead).
	TOTAL

20 BODY POSITION & FOOTWORK INVENTORY

Body position and footwork problems can be very quickly improved. In this category, you will assess how well you use body position and court position to your advantage. Score yourself as follows:

Always-5, Usually-4, Sometimes-3, Seldom-2, Never-1.

Add your scores: 24-3.0, 28-3.5, 32-4.0, 35-4.5, 38-5.0

	I keep my shoulders over my feet, instead of bending at the waist.
	I move to the 7 ft. line quickly at the first good opportunity.
	When moving forward, I pause as my opponent hits the ball.
	I move my feet to get into a well-balanced position to hit balls within my "comfort zone," instead of reaching for balls.
	I keep my shoulders square with oncoming balls, except for return of serve. (Hitting from a sideways position ONLY on return of serve to generate power and depth.)

	I understand shading; and always protect the middle when ball is diagonally/cross-court from me.
	I extend my paddle to the ball & lead with the tip (instead of keeping my paddle parallel to the ground) when volleying, dinking, or hitting a drop shot.
	I return my paddle to a (backhand) ready position between shots.
	TOTAL

Now, list each total below and add them together to determine your skill level:

DECISION MAKING INVENTORY	
SHOT-MAKING INVENTORY	
BODY POSITION & FOOTWORK INVENTORY	
TOTAL	
SKILL LEVEL	

Your skill level (if you've scored each item honestly*) will be as follows:

67	–	79	**3.0**
80	–	92	**3.5**
93	–	104	**4.0**
105	–	115	**4.5**
116	–		**5.0**

*many players either under-rate or over-rate themselves. You may need to check some of the items out with a certified instructor, or with someone who plays with and against you often if you have doubts. Your goal is to be accurate; so take plenty of time with your assessments. A 0-2 score on any item could move you to a lower skill level.

PART THREE
"The Journey to the Top of the Podium"

Becoming a winning tournament player requires sacrifice and commitment. Having worked my way to the top of the podium all the way to the national level, I can testify to the hard work, setbacks, and daily renewal of my commitment to keep drilling, remain coachable, and enjoy the process toward my goals.

Part Three is all about "fine-tuning" techniques and strategies, understanding positioning and movement during points, and drilling with attitude and purpose. The "Ladder To Success" emphasizes efficient body position on all shots to minimize physical stress and promote endurance throughout long events which can last several hours.

Singles is a great way to improve conditioning for doubles play, and with the proper understanding of singles strategies, is not as difficult as many believe. Many of these strategies are included in this section.

Finally, the subject of coaching, and how to find a qualified coach. Even though I am a trained and certified teaching professional, I couldn't adequately train myself. I needed on-the-spot observation and critique from someone who knew my strengths and weaknesses and how to direct me toward success. The view from the top of the podium is beautiful, and I would never have experienced that view without my coach's expertise. It's the best decision I could have made!

21 LADDER TO SUCCESS

As with any ladder, we begin at the bottom and climb our way to the top. At the bottom of the game of pickleball, we find the most neglected piece of the game—our feet. Footwork is the foundation of successful play; with efficient and active footwork, we can reach our full potential. Without it, our success will be limited.

Next, we take a look at body position. Knees are first; are they bent enough to keep you over your feet? If not, the result is to bend at the waist which compromises balance and invites back injuries. Are your shoulders in line with your knees and toes? If so, you are well on your way up the ladder. While we are looking at body position, it is also most efficient to keep the shoulders square with the ball, rather than sideways—except on the return of serve (returning serve from a sideways position will generate additional power and result in a deeper return with less effort).

Now that your feet are active, your knees are bent, and your shoulders are in line with weight on your toes with very little bend in the waist, you are ready to apply efficient technique and control on all shots.

Equally important to your footwork is your mental game. It takes time to learn and practice all the possible shots; but you must also know how to use them and when to use them most efficiently. Once you have learned how to "size-up" your opponent, and what your best shot selection in every situation is, you will increase your wins, and reduce your errors dramatically.

Now, combine all 5 steps on the ladder, and you are ready to climb to the "top of the ladder" and the "top of the winner's podium!"

WINNER!

5. Am I making good shot selection and mental decisions?

4. Is my technique efficient on all 8 shots?

3. Are my shoulders over my toes and square with the ball after return?

2. Are my knees bent, weight over shoes

1. Are my feet active?

THESE STEPS ARE IN ORDER OF IMPORTANCE, BEGINNING WITH FOOTWORK.

MY PERSONAL "LADDER TO SUCCESS" WORKSHEET

After reading and understanding the first 3 steps on your "ladder," you need to condition your body to apply these steps to your personal success. The following drills will build upper leg strength, which is essential for improving control and reducing errors on all shots. For most, this is difficult and will take daily repeating for 2-4 weeks.

The "sit-on-it" drill: assume a sitting position, making sure your weight is over your toes and your shoulders are in line with your knees and toes. Hold this position for 15 seconds, or until your upper legs begin 'screaming' at you. Rest for 1 minute, then repeat twice. As you do this each day, your time will improve to 30 seconds or more. This will make it easy to stay down and balanced during points; and the extra upper leg strength will reduce stress on your knees. The result: better control, and less injuries.

My progress:

The "sit-and-move" drills:

Assume the sitting position, and move your feet in place for 10 seconds, counting your steps. 30 is good; 40 is better; 50+ is excellent.

Sitting position with side-stepping movement from the left sideline to the right sideline, and back. Repeat twice, or stop if any pain occurs, and rest before repeating again.

Sitting position, quickly moving both feet inside 7-ft line, and both feet behind 7-ft line for 10 seconds. Repeat twice as in #2. Caution! When stepping backward, make sure to keep your shoulders over your toes, and your knees bent.

My progress:

The "two-handed-catch" drill (requires 2 players): Assume the sitting position at the 7-ft line, with practice partner in sitting position on opposite side of the net at the 7-ft line. Toss balls into the 7-ft zone, making your partner move to the ball. Stay square to the ball, and catch it with both hands and freeze (pausing to check if you stayed in correct position during the catch). This drill incorporates steps 1, 2, and 3 on your ladder.

My progress:

THE BAD NEWS – Initially, these drills will make your upper legs and calf muscles feel overused and sore. If this is the case, congratulate yourself for a great workout! If not, get back on the court and do them again. "No pain, no gain."

THE GOOD NEWS – If practiced faithfully, your pain will be replaced with new strength and quickness on the court; and your success will increase rapidly.

(END)

Pat Carroll

STEP 4: EFFICIENT TECHNIQUE ON ALL MY SHOTS

SERVE – Stand sideways to your target, assume sitting position, and shift weight from back foot to front foot; leaning into the ball at contact. Contact should be made in front of your forward foot.

My progress:

RETURN OF SERVE – Move feet and assume a sideways position with paddle back and ready to stroke forward. Stay down, and step with the front foot, contacting the ball in front in sitting position. It is very beneficial to lean into your return, which will generate more power, and naturally move your body forward to the 7-ft line. Maintain sitting position throughout the shot. Do not straighten up while approaching the line!

67

My progress:

DINKS, VOLLEYS, AND DROP SHOTS – Remain in the sitting position throughout the point while at the 7-ft line, remembering to stay square with the ball (as in the 2-handed catch drill) and set feet before the hit, NEVER moving feet during the hit. There is plenty of time, if your feet remain active.

My progress:

STEP 5: GOOD SHOT SELECTION AND COURT MANAGEMENT

After doing your "decision-making and shot-selection inventory," you will discover how successful each shot is when your body is properly balanced and moving efficiently. Using the "shading" method of court management, always moving with the ball when it's on the opponent's side and staying square to the ball in sitting position will close off all easy shots from your opponent and result in many more points won easily.

Finally, **COMMUNICATION** is essential for winning play. Whether you are a member of a competitive doubles team, or playing for fun with different partners, finding your voice and using it will add more success to your game. After all, it IS doubles, right?

My progress:

22 COURT POSITION AND MOVEMENT

Move with the ball (it's called "shading")

The purpose of "shading" is to cover the court most efficiently, and to protect the middle. The person on the diagonal from the ball (when it's on the opponent's side) is responsible for 2/3 of the court, especially the middle.

(Use the "pie slice" method to determine position.)

Shading from the Non-volley line

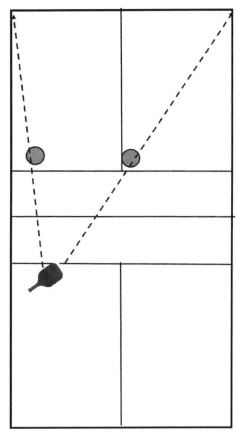

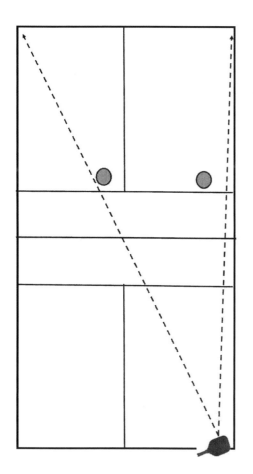

Shading from the back court

"Shading" takes away an opponent's straight shots, down-the-middle shots, and leaves difficult angle shots.

For a good visual, stretch a line from the hitter to each corner of the opposite court. Players must be positioned touching the line on their respective side.

It is important to remember that the partner on the same half of the court as the hitter should remain **still**, allowing partner to take all shots except those that come directly to him/her.

Get as close as you can to the 7 ft line—
don't play 3 feet back

Whose Ball Is It?????

Use shading always and THE MIDDLE BALL BELONGS TO THE PLAYER ON THE SIDE THE BALL IS MOVING TOWARD. Sooooooo:

Who takes 'middle' on 3rd shot (returned serve)?
THE SERVER

Drill: Dinking with movement—MOVE WITH THE BALL! Keep the ball in front of you.

23 WINNING DOUBLES: "PLAYING WITH A PLAN"

The main ingredient in doubles is your plan. In order to form your plan and succeed, both team members must understand and agree on the following basics:

More than 85% of all points are won on errors, not winners. This is why the team that focuses on the middle rather than sidelines for most shots is most likely to win the game.

As the receiving team, your job is to PREVENT THE SERVING TEAM FROM SCORING. We MUST keep our returns deep (preferably down the middle), and get to the line asap. Once you are in, choose targets even with the feet of the opponent with the intention of causing them to hit "up" on the ball. Be patient and keep on dinking until you get the high ball to put away. Frequently, you will "out-patience" the opponent, causing them to make impatient shots which either result in errors or easy put-aways for you and your partner.

As the serving team, your challenge is to get to the line safely, and DIFFUSE THE RECEIVING TEAM'S ADVANTAGE in getting to that line first. This begins with a deep serve to increase the chance of a short return. Next, plan on hitting a soft, low cross-court shot into the non-volley zone so your partner can get to the line (one in is better than none in). Without a "drop-shot" approach, both of you need to stay back until after the 3rd shot has been hit, giving the receiving team a greater advantage. This results in relying on opponents' errors to score points. It's much more satisfying to construct points with a good plan and drop shot; followed with lots of patience and discipline at the line.

FIND YOUR VOICE AND USE IT! The team that communicates on every shot prevents confusion on the court, and creates efficient court management. Talking to your partner reinforces your plan; and wins more points.

BE EAGER TO "SET UP" YOUR PARTNER WITH EVERY SHOT. The best doubles team includes teammates who choose shots which keep their partner safe, and can potentially set up their partner for winning shots. Use the "shading method" of court management, choosing the best shot for the set-up. A high percentage of these set-up shots will be dinks and/or drop shots.

24 THE DIFFERENCE BETWEEN WINNERS AND "OTHERS"

...IS IN HOW YOU PREPARE FOR YOUR MATCH

THE SEVEN "P's" FOR SUCCESS

Proper

Prior

Preparation

Prevents

Poor

Pickleball

Performance

Many competitive players enter the court for their match with little or no thought to conditions of the weather, courts, and type of ball. **IF CONDITIONS ARE NOT IDEAL, LOSERS COMPLAIN AND WINNERS ADJUST!**

Knowing the difference in surfaces can prevent unnecessary frustration.

- On outdoor courts there can be big differences in the bounce of the ball. A rougher surface is described as "slow," and will cause the ball to slow after the bounce and at times it will set up for the hit. This requires awareness that you will need to move closer to the bounce in order to hit the shot with optimum balance and control. A smoother surface, described as "fast," can cause the ball to actually skid off the bounce and stay lower. This requires that you will need to allow a greater distance between the bounce and your contact with the hit. Balls most often used on outdoor courts will have a relatively hard surface with small holes to reduce the affects of wind. Cold weather will increase the pace of the ball, and warm weather will slow the ball.

- Indoor courts are usually a wooden gymnasium surface and will often be much faster than outdoor courts. For this reason, there are balls designed specifically with softer surfaces and larger holes to reduce the speed off the bounce.

- Windy conditions require more rapid footwork, and choosing larger targets for your shots. Be aware of the wind direction when selecting which end of the court you want to start the match. If it is a side wind, I will prefer to start on the end which blows toward my forehand (simply because I have more reach with my forehand). This choice puts my opponents on the end where the wind will be blowing the ball toward and away from their backhand, where they have less reach. Also keep in mind whether you and your opponents are right-handed or left-handed. If it is blowing in the direction of the court, most players will choose to play with the wind rather than against it; but I find that the soft game is easier when playing against the wind. This should depend on personal preference of you and your partner.

Now that you have properly prepared for the conditions of your match, it's time to "size up your opponents."

25 SIZING UP OPPONENTS' STRENGTHS & WEAKNESSES

One of the most unproductive practices I've witnessed in recent years is a doubles team using their match warm-up time hitting with each other instead of hitting with their opponents. Where is the benefit in hitting with someone whose shots you will never need to react to? Realistically, this is not a warm up. It's too short. If you haven't done at least a 30-minute warm up previous to the match, you are truly not ready to play. So, get on the same side with your partner during those few precious minutes you have and start "sizing up your opponents." There is no rule as yet which requires that you warm up on the same side together; but once the starting serving team and side have been determined it seems obvious that each team should proceed on their own side of the net. "Smart" teams will demand to stay on the same side.

The best opportunity to evaluate your opponents is in warming up with them before the game begins, or watch them play before you join them in a game. If this isn't possible, it will be necessary to observe your opponent during play with the following guidelines. Then, COMMUNICATE YOUR OBSERVATIONS WITH YOUR PARTNER, AND ADJUST YOUR GAME PLAN ACCORDINGLY.

At the 7 ft. Line

Do they favor the forehand or backhand dink? Plan to use forcing shots to their weakest side.

If they stand in one place and reach for shots, they will demonstrate poor footwork on shots hit away from them.

If they turn sideways to hit dinks or volleys rather than staying square with the shot, their recovery time will be slower.

From the Baseline

Observe whether they favor the forehand or backhand strokes. Avoid their strongest side when possible.

If they don't warm up drop shots, expect them to over hit their 3rd shot, and be ready to hit lots of volleys from the 7 ft. line.

If they stay 2 feet or more behind the 7 ft. line, or are slow to approach on their return of serve, soft shots even with their feet will be effective.

Serving and Returning Serve

If their serve and/or return of serve is consistently short (more than 3 feet from your baseline), it will be much easier to hit forcing shots on your own returns and drop shots. A low, hard serve is easier to return than a higher, softer serve.

IMPORTANT! DON'T ALLOW YOUR OPPONENTS TO "SEDUCE" YOU INTO THEIR HARD GAME. DINKS AND DROP SHOTS ARE ESSENTIAL TO CONSTRUCTING POINTS.

26 LOOKING FOR THE PERFECT DOUBLES PARTNER?

In all my years of being coached, I was never coached on what to look for when selecting a partner. At first, I was an unknown player and had to settle for tournament directors matching me with a partner or choose from a published list of players without partners. I call these "pot luck" partners. This is very difficult, since there is little or no opportunity to play together or get to know each other before the actual doubles event. I didn't end up on the podium in these cases, but I definitely learned a lot about what I wanted and "didn't" want in a partner.

Finding the perfect partner is perhaps the biggest challenge for the tournament player, regardless of your skill and experience. Initially, my only priority was to find the highest skilled player who was willing to play with me, to improve our chances of winning. Today, the highest skilled player is not as important to me as finding the partner I "like" who has the desire to work together and discover our potential as a team.

Having been rated 5.0 and won many titles in doubles, I now have more opportunities to double-up with highly skilled players; but will always require the following priorities:

- **Integrity**. Winning is important, but honesty is more important.
- **Open-minded**. Agrees on most strategies and is willing to compromise on others.
- **Communication**. Willing to speak up, and able to listen.
- **Always focusing** on setting up and/or protecting each other.
- **A sense of humor**. Doesn't take himself/herself too seriously.
- **Mental toughness**. Able to focus on and stay with our game plan.
- **Skill level**. Potential is more important than a higher skill level if all the above priorities are present.

These are my own priorities. Yours may be different, but it is important to know what they are. Sharing your priorities can be extremely beneficial in understanding each other and building a more effective partnership.

27 MIXED DOUBLES PARTNERING

Involves Added Dynamics!

Frequently, mixed doubles includes unequal skill levels. The male is usually physically stronger and more aggressive, which means the female will be targeted for most shots. This can cause the male to lose patience, poach, and overhit, which puts the female at a disadvantage.

The best mixed doubles teams play as equals, with awareness of each others' strengths and how to exploit them. Since the player on the diagonal from the opponent's shot should cover more than half of the court, the weaker player will set up the stronger partner by hitting straight shots to the opponents. Thus, the stronger partner has more opportunities to cover the shots. The stronger partner should hit more cross-court shots to be in position to cover more return shots.

In the 2012 Nationals, I was fortunate to play for the first time with Phil Dunmeyer (his partner and my partner were injured and we were allowed to partner for the tournament). Even though we had never played a single game together, we played as if we had played together for years, and won the tournament without losing a game. Phil is the best partner I have had, and we have had many wins together. Most importantly, he possesses every quality on my priority list. He's the strongest player physically, so I want to set him up as much as possible; however, he never takes my shots and we communicate with each other on every shot. He has been my best teacher of what I need in a partner.

Be patient in your search for the perfect partner, and learn more about what works and doesn't work for you in your experiences of playing with "pot luck" partners. Keep on improving your own skills, know your priorities, and look for "Quality first, and Skill second." That perfect partner is hopefully doing the same, preparing for the day when you both meet on the court!

28 COMMUNICATION: FIND YOUR VOICE AND USE IT!

To play successful doubles, especially with a partner that you've never played with before, it is essential to communicate. Failure to communicate frequently causes one or all of the following results:

- Both players go for the same shot, causing an error.
- Neither player goes for the shot, which results in confusion, attempted mind-reading, frustration, and loss of points and games.

Communication During Points

For many, using your voice is one of the most difficult parts of the game. Speaking up can feel like "coaching," unless it's done productively. Speak asap, before the ball has bounced. BOTH partners should use their voices for best results.

- Using words like "yours" or "mine" on most shots, even the ones which are obvious, keeps you connected with your partner; and very importantly, keeps your voice active for the shots which need communication.

- Some other forms of communicating can be, "I'm here" (to inform your partner of your location on the court), "Go-go-go" (to encourage your partner to reach a difficult shot), "you got it" (expresses confidence in your partner).

Communication Between Points

- It is very important to form a "plan" with your partner.
- Agree on who will take the "down-the-middle" return if you're the serving team.
- Select the partner to take most drop shots.
- Share observations of the opponents' strengths and weaknesses, etc.

MOST IMPORTANT—PRAISE AND ENCOURAGE EACH OTHER

29 SINGLES, ANYONE?

The key to winning singles in pickleball begins, of course, with "footwork." Obviously, movement is of prime importance when you are covering the entire court. With efficient footwork and proper shot selection, covering the court becomes much easier.

ERRORS, ERRORS, ERRORS!!!

Whether it's singles or doubles, at every level of play, 85% of points are lost due to errors; which means that only a mere 15% are earned by winning shots.

Between highly skilled players, errors are usually a result of the opponent's accurate placement. Unforced errors are a significant part of every match, usually due to a poor choice of shots or faulty technique. If you can reduce your unforced errors and force a few from your opponent, your wins will increase significantly.

SO, HOW DO I REDUCE MY ERRORS?

- The "worst" error is to hit into the net; so the first task on every shot is to clear the net. If you and your opponent are both at the baseline, aim your shot two to four feet above the net to create a good margin for error and insure deep shots.

- Make your targets at least one foot (two or three is safer) inside the lines to give yourself good margin for error.

- Whenever you are in trouble during a point and forced to play a defensive shot, aim your shot high, deep, and cross-court to allow more time to recover for the next shot. If the opponent is at the 7-foot line, aim high over the opponent's reach.

- Early in the point, hit your shots DEEP cross-court or DEEP down the middle. This reduces your chance of error and keeps your opponent on the defense.

- Movement to the ball and early preparation are the keys to consistent strokes. On ground strokes (meaning the ball has bounced into your court before you contact it) hit every ball in your "comfort zone," about waist high, and be balanced and SET at contact. Unlike the "push" shots in doubles, a step forward from a sideways position into the shot will generate more power and depth.

- It is usually safer to direct a ball back to the direction it came from rather than changing the angle. Only change the direction of a ball that you can control and are in good position to attack.

STRATEGY: "PLAY WITH A PLAN!"

1. **Hit to the open court**: Once you have developed your skills to the level where you can consistently direct most shots over the net and into the court, you are ready to aim the ball away from your opponent. Because your opponent cannot cover all possible angles at once, there will always be an opening. You may be able to hit the ball out of his/her reach for a winning shot. At the very least, you will force him/her to run to the ball and complicate his/her return shot. Your chances of hitting a winning shot increase significantly when you approach to the 7-foot line, because your opponent will have less time to react and chase down your shot.

2. **Hit behind your opponent**: During a point, your opponent will expect you to aim for the open court, particularly if you've managed to hit some forcing shots

or even outright winners. As your opponent begins to anticipate your shot and perhaps lean a bit in that direction, you should direct your next shot behind him/her. He/she will find it extremely difficult to change direction, regain his/her balance, and adjust to the oncoming ball. This strategy is most effective against players who are very quick at moving side to side. It also works well when you have drawn your opponent very wide to one side, and he/she is hustling back toward the center of the court to protect the wide-open court.

3. **Move your opponent around the court**: Mixing up your shots by varying speed, depth, and placement will challenge your opponent on every point. Presenting your opponent with a wide variety of shots that are well disguised keeps him/her confused and off balance. Even if your opponent is able to respond to your placements, chances are that over time, he/she will become fatigued and unable to reach a few balls.

At most levels of playing skill, the secret of moving your opponent around the court is to include up and back movement along with the more typical side-to-side moves. You might find it effective to begin the point with a deep baseline shot, followed by a short angle or a drop shot that forces him/her to move forward at full speed. Your next shot can be a drive to the other side or perhaps a lob over his/her head. After a few all-out sprints up and back and side to side, you have sent the message that your opponent is in for a difficult match.

4. **Discover your opponents weaknesses, and exploit them**: If you discover, for example, that your opponent has a weak, defensive backhand, direct serves and ground strokes to the backhand until he/she presents you with an error or a weak shot that you can attack.

5. **Adjust to the conditions**: Sun, wind, temperature, and humidity all affect the play in matches. Experience in coping with these conditions is invaluable, so you have to practice and play in all kinds of weather. You'll learn how to keep the ball in the court by hitting away from the direction of the wind if it is blowing across the court. Drop shots work well with the wind in your face; and lobs can be very affective in windy conditions (only if you have good lobbing skill).

TECHNIQUE: How does it differ from doubles technique?

In doubles play, there are mostly only two shots which involve a backswing: the return of serve, and the overhead. Since the goal in doubles is primarily to get to the 7-foot line, nearly all shots are "pushes," keeping the paddle in front of the body throughout the shot.

In singles, many shots will be hit from close to the baseline (until the opportunity to approach to the 7-foot line). These shots are executed similar to the return of serve, with a backswing and a follow-through to create good depth into the opponent's court.

One of the most common errors in singles technique is taking too big a backswing and attempting to "over-power" the ball. It's great, when it works; but due to the small size of the court, smaller backswings will produce plenty of power, plus control and consistency. Combine the smaller backswing with a more exaggerated follow through and you will accomplish great power, control, and consistency; plus less errors.

NOW IT'S TIME TO PUT ALL THIS INFORMATION INTO "PRACTICE!"

"Practice" is the key to success; the following are some drills designed to create and reinforce simple plans and patterns for many playing situations and opposing playing styles. If they are practiced and applied to your singles game, your success level will improve.

- Mark a line with tape or chalk 5 ft. in from the baseline. Hit ground strokes with the intention of bouncing the ball beyond the 5 ft. line. If your hitting partner hits a ball short of the 5 ft. line, approach the net in the direction of your approach shot and play the point out.

- Bounce and hit your approach shot, always following the ball and positioning yourself in the center of the shaded area from the ball to the corners of your court. Play the point out.

- With 3 people, 2 remain at the baseline while the singles player stays at the 7-ft. line. The object is to pass the singles player. Active feet and "shading" are essential for the single during this drill.

- 3 or 4 people working on changing direction of the ball. Player 1 goes cross-court to player 2; 2 goes down-the-

94

line to player 3; 3 goes cross-court to player 4; 4 goes down-the-line to player 1; and the drill continues.

- Another variation of the previous drill is to hit successive down-the-line shots from each side of the court; and successive cross-court shots from each side of the court.

My *"Formula for Success" Is:*

- To maintain your skill level—15 minutes practice before every singles play day.
- To raise your skill level—for every 2 hours of singles play, 30 minutes should be practice and drills. Practice hard, reduce those errors, and enjoy winning!

30 MORE THAN "ONE REASON" TO DRILL?

Most of us limit our success with the "attitude" we bring onto the court. Changing takes time; and the first step is to discover negative thoughts that need to be changed; and positive thoughts to replace them.

Soooo, the first reason to drill is obvious: we want to improve our shots, gaining more control and consistency, and win more and lose less.

The second reason, and for many the MOST IMPORTANT reason, is to train our minds to focus productively. Here are a few examples of "non-productive" thinking, which ultimately leads to errors:

1. Focusing on "who" I'm playing.
2. Planning to "hit a winner" on EVERY shot.
3. Dwelling on previous errors.
4. Blaming our partner for lost points.*

These mental errors can be replaced with "productive" thinking, which needs to be practiced; it's "simple," but "not easy" to change:

1. Focus on "enjoying the BALL," watching it through the hit.

2. Plan on "constructing" the point, setting up your partner for the win whenever possible (doubles games are won by "teams," not "individuals").

3. STAY WHERE YOUR FEET ARE (Don't "live in the past")!

4. Your partner is "human" AND SO ARE YOU!!*

*When your opponent has hit a winner, briefly review the point to determine where you or your partner began setting up the point for your opponent:

- Did you "overhit" as described in #2?

- Was your shot too short, or hit into the "comfort zone" of your opponent?

- Determine a "positive solution," and make it your plan.

Suggested Footwork Drills

1. Set a timer for 10 seconds; move your feet in place at least 30 times within the 10 seconds.

2. Set again and shuffle at 7-foot line from one side to the other and back. See how far you get in 10 seconds.

3. Try drills #1 and #2 using 10 second timer to see how far you get.

4. Using a stop watch, see how many seconds it takes you to complete drill #3.

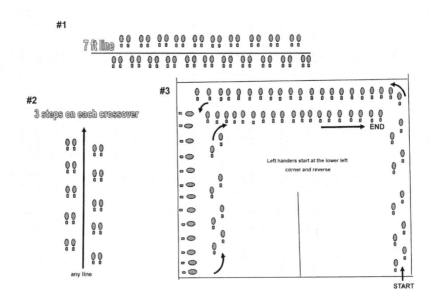

SCORE YOUR SUCCESS

	Week 1	Week 2	Week 3
FOOTWORK TECHNIQUE			
Active feet?			
Best time			
DINK DRILLS			
Personal best			
DROP SHOT DRILLS			
12 ft line			
18 ft line			
Serve & 3rd shot			
TECHNIQUE for dinks and/or drop shots (grade yourself, A to F)			
Contact within "comfort zone"?			
Push—no backswing!			
Paddle in front?			
Paddle tip aimed DOWN?			
VOLLEYS			
Placement drills			
TECHNIQUE			
Backhand ready			
70% backhands			

Push—no swinging			
LOBS (count for # of successful lobs in-a-row from 7 ft. line)			
Beyond 18' line			
TECHNIQUE			
Keep ball well out in front, with high follow-through			
OVERHEADS (# of successful shots in-a-row)			
Personal best			
TECHNIQUE			
Sideways position, opposite arm pointing up, contact ball out in front, at optimal height of reach.			
Hitting a high volley, square with the ball, is also effective.			
Don't overplay overheads; 'down the middle' is safe and effective.			
ATTITUDE: (see "non-productive thinking" vs. "productive thinking")			
Indicate #'s which NEED improvement, along with a grade. The goal is to see progress in attitude each week.			
NOTES:			

31 PAT'S GUIDE FOR DRILLS

- 10 min – stretch & warm-up.

- 15 min – footwork drills: record best time.

- 15 min – Cross-court dink drills: record best total.

- 15 min – drops drills at 12 & 18 ft lines: record best at 18 ft line.

- 20 min – serve, return, & 3rd shot: 3 tries for each server, then repeat for 10 minutes; record best success on 3rd shot (MUST land in kitchen to count).

- 15 min – Play points, with "NMW" (NO MATTER WHAT) drop shot from back of 7 ft line.

- 10 min – Summary, questions & answers, and complete sheet for week 1.

Week 2

- 10 min – stretch & warm-up.

- 10 min – Footwork drills: record best time.

- 10 min – Dink Drills, 2 on 1: record best total when "1."

- 15 min – Drops Drills at 12 & 18 ft lines; minimum 5 in a row at 12 to advance to 18 ft line, then record total at 18 ft line.

- 15 min – Serve, return, & 3rd shot: 3 tries for each server, then repeat for 10 minutes; record best success on 3rd shot (MUST land in kitchen to count).

- 15 min – Volleys – straight across, rotate right every 90 seconds; record best total.

- 20 min – Play points, with "NMW" drop shot from back of 7 ft line, and "DINKS," unless ball is above knees.

- 10 min – Summary, questions & answers, score your success on week 2.

Week 3

- 10 min – Stretch & warm-up.

- 30 min – Record your success after each dril.l

- 5 min – Footwork drills & time.

- 5 min – Dinks – straight.

- 5 – Drops – from 18 ft line.

- 7 min – Serve & Drop on 3rd shot.

- 7 min – Volleys – 2 on 1 & rotate.

- 10 min – Lobs from baseline; count # of successive lobs (MUST land beyond 18 ft line to count) and record.

- 10 min – Overheads: feed lobs to partner, keeping them short (between 12 ft & 18 ft). Record successive overheads (MUST land beyond 18 ft line and on same side as "lobber").

- 10 min – Play points as in Week 2.

- 10 min – Summary, questions & answers; record success totals.

THE RESULTS OF "PRODUCTIVE" DRILLS

If you have been productively focused in practicing the drills introduced throughout this process, you will find yourself playing with a new consciousness of what you need to do to achieve your goals in pickleball. The process of achieving these goals can be frustrating, and even a little discouraging at times; but if you continually renew your commitment to regular practice sessions, using the suggested simple "counting" and tracking your best totals, those goals CAN and WILL be reached!

Throughout the process, you have discovered that you can drill on Dinks, Volleys, Drop Shots, Lobs, Overheads, and the "ever-important" Footwork; and do it all within one hour. Schedule time each week for these drills, concentrating on the areas you need the most work on.

32 PAT'S PICKLOSOPHY 90-DAY PLAN

I, _____, am committed
to accomplishing the following goals within the next 90 days
*(check only the goals you are willing to commit to):

1. _____Make my backhand my most reliable shot,
   especially at the 7-foot line.
2. _____Improve my footwork, always moving my feet
   before my paddle.
3. _____Develop and use a drop shot whenever my
   opponents are in, and I'm not.
4. _____Accomplish at least 30 dinks in a row.
5. _____Serve 100% of 10 serves in; and 70% deep (within
   5 ft. of the baseline).
6. _____(other) _____

My long-term goals are:
1. _____To raise my skill level from _____ to _____.
2. _____To win a medal in competition.
3. _____To play with confidence in all levels of open play.

My plan for achieving all the above goals is:

1. _____ Practice 15 minutes before each play day.
2. _____ Practice 10 minutes before each play day.
3. _____ Practice 5 minutes before each play day.
4. _____ Other _____

Signed _____ Date _____

*Set up a reminder on your calendar to review these commitments 90 days from the above date. If you have done everything you've committed to, you will be very happy with your results....

33 COACHING

If you want to raise the level of your game and look better doing it, you need occasional coaching from a qualified pro.

There are times when you are at the top of your game and feel like you are doing everything right. But you really aren't doing everything right—nobody's perfect. There are aspects of your game that can be tweaked to make you play even better. You need a pro to tweak your game so you can move up in ranking, and look better doing it.

I'm a trained and certified teaching professional who has won gold medals in all events, but there are times when I need help. I hired a coach who lives hundreds of miles away. I see him as often as I can because he sees parts of my game that need adjusting. My pro accelerates improvements in my game. If I tried to be my own coach, it would take me a lot longer to figure out my problems and I would waste a lot of time doing it.

Choosing your coach will be one of the most important choices you make for improving your game. Listening to an unqualified instructor can limit your potential; but worse yet, it can result in injury.

Advice from instructors/fellow players comes from a well-meaning place; however, it takes years of study and training to become a qualified coach. It may sound easy, but competing/playing vs coaching requires knowledge beyond the understanding of how to win points.

In the 1980's I trained for coaching as an apprentice under a top rated professional for six months. I then had to attend a full day of written and on-court testing, followed by teaching lessons in front of certified professional judges. I was delighted to receive my certification and impressed with the extensive scrutinizing involved in qualifying to be a professional instructor. Periodic future testing was also required to show that I maintained my teaching and playing skills and had stayed current on teaching techniques as they continued to change and improve.

In 2004, I began my transition from a tennis player to a pickleball player and realized that my tennis skills would not work without coaching. I chose a great coach, and committed to practicing every day to master the new techniques. After a long process I felt ready and qualified to teach pickleball, but continued with coaching sessions from my coach. Thanks to his strategies and efficient techniques, I won 8 National Championships in Singles, Doubles, and Mixed Doubles plus gold medals in nearly every additional tournament I entered. I have also traveled several thousand miles in 2015 and 2016 teaching and promoting pickleball throughout the USA. After over 13 years of coaching and playing pickleball, I am still a student of the sport and am still learning!

Experience and skill level of instructors is important; but it's most essential that your coach has had sufficient training and certification to be a qualified teaching professional. There are some great qualified coaches out there; but there are many more who claim to be but haven't put in the time and work to fully understand the difference between playing and teaching the game. Don't hesitate to ask for your prospective coach's credentials.

34 IN CONCLUSION

It always seems like there should be more to the game than the previous pages. Frankly, there IS more, but my experience has taught me that keeping the game simple results in less errors, more control, and greater success. This is why I give little importance to spins and fancy shots. Efficiency is the goal, and "Less Is More!"

In recent years there has been a huge number of tennis players learning pickleball; many very skilled, who have been and will continue to attempt to change pickleball to exclusively a power game. I am happy to say that the highest skilled doubles tournaments are still being won by the players who have mastered the soft dinks and drop shots, and play with the most patience and discipline.

The growth of pickleball in the USA has been phenomenal in recent years, largely due to the USA Pickleball Association's Ambassador Program. This is a group of volunteers organized in the early 2000s with Earl Hill as the program's creator and original director. These carefully selected ambassadors are passionate and dedicated to introducing and promoting pickleball; and have increased in number from less than 100 to thousands, located all over our country. Whether you are a competitive tournament player, or one who plays for the fun and exercise, please consider becoming a member of the USA Pickleball Association. They are doing such great work preserving the integrity of our sport, providing lists of places to play all over the country, and assisting new organizations in starting their own pickleball program. The membership fee is a bargain, with many benefits; plus you'll get a free shirt, and most importantly, you will be supporting the continued growth of pickleball! Just go online to USAPA.org to join.

At age 75 I continue to teach and play at a high level. I'm no longer playing at the 5.0 skill level, and can see a finish line; but I have a much better chance to play another 10+ years as long as I remain committed to keeping the game SIMPLE and SMART—the way it was created to be....

"THE BEGINNING"

For information regarding clinics and private
instruction, email: *pickleballpat@yahoo.com*
"Have Paddle - Will Travel"

Made in the USA
San Bernardino, CA
14 May 2019